THE NAVAJO LONG WALK

Thanks to Robert J. Early, who commissioned a magazine article that served
as the germ of this book. Thanks also to Johnson Dennison, Teddy Draper,
Robert Roessel, Ruth Roessel, Monty Roessel, and Harry Walters for their
generous help in research.

RIO NUEVO PUBLISHERS®
P.O. Box 5250, Tucson, Arizona 85703-0250
(520) 623-9558, www.rionuevo.com

Cover and Interior Design: Karen Schober, Seattle, Washington

                    Library of Congress Cataloging-in-Publication Data
Cheek, Larry.
The Navajo Long Walk / Lawrence W. Cheek.
     p. cm. -- (Look West series)
 Includes bibliographical references.
ISBN 1-887896-65-1 (hardcover)
1. Navajo Long Walk, 1863-1867. 2. Navajo Indians--Relocation. 3. Navajo
Indians--Government relations. 4. Indians, Treatment of--Southwest, New--History--19th
century. I. Title. II. Series: Look West.
E99.N3C46 2004
978.9004'9726--dc22
                              2004010474
Printed in Hong Kong
10 9 8 7 6 5 4 3 2 1

THE
NAVAJO
LONG WALK

Lawrence W. Cheek

LOOK WEST
SERIES

RIO NUEVO PUBLISHERS
TUCSON, ARIZONA

Chinle Wash near the mouth of Canyon de Chelly.

WE DRIVE ON WATER, ON A SHEET OF
MILK-CHOCOLATE SPRING RUNOFF THAT RIPPLES
THROUGH CANYON DEL MUERTO FROM ONE WALL TO THE
OTHER. IT'S A RIVER THREE INCHES DEEP AND A HUNDRED
FEET WIDE, MINED WITH QUICKSAND AMBUSHES—WHOSE
LOCATIONS, FORTUNATELY, TEDDY DRAPER SR. LONG AGO
MEMORIZED, SO HE CAN DIRECT US SAFELY AROUND. HE WAS
BORN IN THIS CANYON SEVENTY-EIGHT YEARS AGO
AND KNOWS IT INTIMATELY.

Draper is guiding photographer Monty Roessel and me to Navajo
Fortress, where he will relate one of the canyon's stories, trickled down
through the generations from his great-great-great-grandmother.
Atop this towering butte, in 1864, a handful of Navajos outwitted a

Above: Chis-Chili, who made the Long Walk as a teenager (1908 portrait by E. A. Burbank).

U.S. Army siege and dodged the holocaust that engulfed the tribe for the next four years, as soldiers gathered and herded at least three-quarters of the tribe to a dismal reservation in east-central New Mexico. Still, Draper jokes affably as we splatter along. "The Navajo people hid easily in this canyon," he says. "Our skin is the same color as the rock."

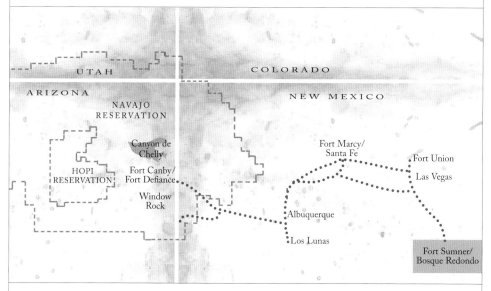

The Army drove the Navajos to Bosque Redondo over several different routes. The longest stretched nearly five hundred miles through Santa Fe and Fort Union.

He laughs, so do I. I've spent enough time among the Navajos to feel comfortable with their wry and prolific humor. Several days will pass before it dawns that his "joke" is as profound as the red canyon's deep and tragic history.

I have come to Canyon del Muerto and its sister, Canyon de Chelly, to begin retracing the route of the Navajos' exile and try to perceive the events through Navajo eyes. The "American" side is easy to research; archives are full of U.S. Army officers' reports and letters, treaties, contemporary newspaper commentaries, and photographs. The Navajo story is harder to follow, although Navajos are not reluctant to talk about this pivotal event in their tribal history. A Navajo narrative can be a swirl of fact and legend, and the storyteller would be insulted if a clueless interviewer tried to pry the pair apart. "Logical contradictions don't matter," explains Roessel, who grew up in the Navajo Nation with a white father and Navajo mother. "A wolf and a rabbit may cooperate to help a human. To a Navajo, it's all true."

There are also cultural minefields to negotiate. Originally I had planned to backpack the 350-mile route of the relocation from Canyon de Chelly in northeastern Arizona to Bosque Redondo in New Mexico. Roessel discussed this scheme with tribal elders and discerned a less-than-warm reception. "It wasn't a hike," one said. A Navajo generally will not tell you directly that you shouldn't do something, but the wise listener will feel a sudden chill. I decided eventually to drive the route, which turned out to be a wise choice for more reasons than one.

With Navajo Fortress in the background, World War II Navajo Code Talker Teddy Draper Sr. relates his family's Long Walk stories.

CANYON OF ROCK, CANYON OF DEATH

The *Diné*, or Navajo people, began filtering into the basins and canyons west of the Chuska Mountains of Arizona and New Mexico in the mid-1700s, claiming an obdurate but lovely land that the Anasazi had deserted some 450 years earlier. The labyrinth of canyons between the Chuska Mountains and the present-day town of Chinle, Arizona, was particularly attractive, and not only for its astounding beauty. Thanks to the permanent streams in the upper reaches of the canyons, the Anasazi and their predecessors, the Basketmakers, had successfully farmed it for a thousand years. The Navajos could do the same.

Trouble, however, came with the territory. Navajos, Utes, and Puebloans skirmished endlessly and raided each other's camps for women and children to press into slavery. In 1805 a Spanish detachment led by Lieutenant Antonio Narbona massacred 115

The term "Anasazi" means "Ancient Enemies" in the Navajo language. Modern Pueblo people, who are descended from these cliff-dwelling people, prefer the term "Ancestral Puebloans."

Navajos huddled in an alcove on a canyon wall with a ricochet rain of thousands of bullets. The name *Canyon del Muerto,* Canyon of the Dead, commemorates the slaughter. (*Cañon de Chelly* was the Spaniards' shot at spelling the Navajo word *tségi,* rock. Today it's commonly pronounced *d'SHAY.*) But not until U.S. Army General James Henry Carleton assumed command of New Mexico Territory in 1862 was the entire Navajo culture threatened with annihilation.

Navajos and Spanish settlers of New Mexico had engaged in a guerrilla war of tit-for-tat raid-and-reprisal for more than two centuries when the U.S. flag rose over the territory in 1846. The Navajo economy was based on sheep, cattle, and slaves, a good many of whom they snatched from Spanish homesteaders. In the Navajo view these were hardly crimes; the Spanish were stealing their traditional grazing lands and hatching deadly alliances with the Navajos' native enemies.

The Americans moved to contain the Navajos with a series of tightening reservation boundaries and treaties that made the Navajos promise to cease hostilities and turn over their raiding "criminals" to the U.S. Army. Peace never survived long. The new U.S.

Mother and child, Bosque Redondo era.

Army presence at Fort Defiance, twenty-five miles south of Canyon de Chelly, was a tumor encroaching on traditional Navajo grazing lands. And the Navajo headmen who signed the treaties could never rein in all the freelance raiding and sniping. The story played out as it always did in the Indian wars: a reel of treachery and misjudgments on both sides, leading to a decisive punch with all the military muscle the U.S. could afford to throw into it.

General Carleton was not a man troubled by indecision or self-doubt. In a photo portrait he sits with arms crossed and jaws clenched into a ferocious scowl. A sympathetic history published in 1935 described him as "a very dynamo of energy, relentless as a chastizer, kindly as an adviser, unwavering in policy but yet comprehensive in the performance, with mind broad enough to see that he was building a state and not merely occupying one-to-be…" A less complimentary appraisal written in 1982 called him an "unscrupulous, ambitious, selfish man, whose bearing radiated an abrasive, tyrannical personality." Add these appraisals together and you have him: dynamic, relentless, abrasive, tyrannical.

Carleton believed the Navajos would understand nothing but the direct application of force, for they were "a people that can be trusted no more than you can trust the wolves that run through their mountains." He also saw himself as a devout Christian and humanitarian,

which was reflected in the plan he devised for the Navajos. Their savage ways would evaporate, he believed, if they were removed from their "haunts, hills, and hiding-places" to a reservation, where they would learn reading, writing, and Christianity. They would then become a "happy and contented people" with no further desire to make war.

Like nearly all white Westerners of the time, Carleton viewed the Navajos and other Native Americans as impediments to progress that had to be subdued and contained. His professed Christian humanitarianism

General James Henry Carleton, 1866.

appears outrageously hypocritical in today's light, but it would not have seemed so in the nineteenth century. He was baptized in

Colonel Christopher "Kit" Carson, 1868.

the doctrine of Manifest Destiny, God's own plan for American democracy to flood the continent. And he was riding a gathering wave of Christian reform that had begun in the 1850s to save the American Indians rather than exterminate them, which had been the de facto government policy. Saving them, of course, did not mean preserving their culture, language, or religion.

Or their homelands. Like any good Manifest Destiny visionary, Carleton had an agenda for Diné-tah, the Navajo heartland. He suspected, as many did, that the Navajo lands held mineral wealth as well as excellent ranch land, and he foresaw a transcontinental railroad straddling the thirty-fifth parallel, which bisects Albuquerque and present-day Flagstaff. Building it would be a difficult proposition in the midst of hostile Navajos.

In retrospect, the American decision to launch an all-out offensive against the Navajos in the middle of its own Civil War seems amazingly reckless, but it reflected the nation's mood. Manifest Destiny was above all a doctrine of moral righteousness, exempt from practical arguments. And the Navajo war might also be seen as an extension of the Union's political determination to firmly reestablish authority all across the continent.

Carleton handed the job of breaking the Navajos' resistance to the most accomplished Indian fighter in the West, Colonel Christopher "Kit" Carson. By then fifty-four and craving a settled domestic life in Taos with his wife and four children, Carson had a diminishing appetite for war. He also had more empathy with and understanding of Indian ways than most soldiers; he had twice married Indian women and adopted Indian orphans. But he had an overriding sense of military duty: whatever his private misgivings, he swallowed them and followed his orders, with the ruthlessness his commander expected.

Carleton established Fort Sumner at what the New Mexicans melodiously called *Bosque Redondo* ("Round Forest," which referred to the cottonwoods beside the Pecos River) in east-central New Mexico. The entire Navajo tribe, which was then estimated at some fifteen thousand people, was to be transplanted there onto forty square miles of prairie, where they would learn modern agriculture quickly enough, Carleton expected, to feed themselves. He ordered Carson to give the Navajos no choices and no room for negotiation:

> Say to them—"Go to the Bosque Redondo, or we will pursue and destroy you. We will not make peace with you on any other terms. You have deceived us too often and robbed and murdered our people too long for us to trust you again at large in your own country. This war shall be pursued against you if it takes years, now that we have begun, until you cease to exist or move. There can be no other talk on the subject."

Canyon de Chelly and Canyon del Muerto formed the Navajos' natural stronghold and sanctuary. From the air the canyon complex looks like the track of a gigantic gnarled crow's foot, deepening as it meanders eastward until the gouge plunges a thousand feet into the plateau. The orange-red de Chelly sandstone is a well-cemented rock that resists lateral weathering, so over some 200 million years the streams have rasped the canyon walls into near-vertical slashes. The broad, sandy bottoms provide beautiful orchard and pasture land. (Captain Albert Pfeiffer grudgingly admired the Navajo efforts at cultivating the canyons, reporting that "the Corn Fields of the Savages are laid out with farmer-like taste…")

As Teddy Draper observed, the canyons also provided thousands of nooks and crannies that the people could melt into, and they could climb like spiders, using hidden trails and tiny holds pecked into the rock that the white men couldn't find. Army troops were justifiably nervous about entering the citadel, and the Navajos knew it. Carleton and Carson decided that a decisive strike in the canyons would break the enemy morale, and that they would launch the attack in the dead of winter, when the Navajos would find it impossible to forage on the run.

In January of 1864, Carson launched a two-pronged assault into the canyons, burning orchards and hogans, taking prisoner those who surrendered and shooting those who didn't. The Navajos offered little effective resistance, apparently because of a shortage of arms, but they hurled rocks and curses. Pfeiffer, commanding the

Canyon del Muerto prong of the attack, wrote matter-of-factly: "Killed two (2) buck Indians and one Squaw who obstinately persisted in hurling rocks and pieces of wood at the soldiers."

The assault worked very well, from the Army point of view. It indeed crushed Navajo morale and raised the spectre of a winter of starvation. Navajo stories tell of people surviving by eating cacti and the heads and feet of horse and sheep carcasses.

Over the next several months thousands of destitute Navajos trudged into Fort Canby (a temporary name for what was called Fort Defiance before and after this period) to surrender. Beginning in February, Army men on horseback began escorting herds of Navajos in wagons and on foot from Fort Canby to Fort Sumner and the Bosque Redondo, forming a ponderous river of humanity that would intermittently flow for more than two years. According to military records, a total of 11,468 Navajos were moved. In tribal history this forced relocation came to be known as the Long Walk.

The spires of Monument Valley, now a Navajo Tribal Park, as seen from Goulding's Trading Post and Museum.

THE TRAIL TO BOSQUE REDONDO

I leave Chinle in my rented Malibu, driving southeast on a cratered tribal road that does not welcome any Chevy without the word "truck" attached. If I'd had the foresight to rent a four-wheel-drive, I might have traced the Long Walk route more precisely, following dirt roads that spiderweb the modern Navajo Nation. Crippled by my sedan mount, I leave the dirt at Fort Defiance and drive mostly over blacktop, nosing out the forts and encampments cited in historical accounts: Fort Wingate, Los Pinos (now named Peralta, twenty miles south of Albuquerque), and of course Fort Sumner.

Anyone trolling for history along this route will be mostly disappointed; this dimension of the story has turned to dust. I cruise around the town of San Rafael, which consists of a bar, a church, and a post office, hunting for Fort Wingate. There's no ruin, no historical marker. I stop at the post office. The postmaster tells me the old fort is "just some dirt now," but gives directions. I drive there and find a few amorphous mounds of dirt, remnants of the adobe fort buildings, behind the inevitable barbed-wire fence and bullet-riddled NO DUMPING sign. Old mattresses, fridges, and water heaters have been dumped. Ten thousand Navajos once camped here, en route to their exile.

A modern Navajo girl sprints across rippled red sand.

Anyone seeking understanding of why the Navajos failed to thrive at Bosque Redondo should see Fort Sumner, however. Or more precisely, its environs. In 1941 the capricious Pecos River changed course and washed the last of the post's adobe architecture toward the Gulf of Mexico. The forest once described as the Bosque Redondo is virtually gone too; the Navajos and soldiers stripped it for firewood in the 1860s. The landscape today is a bleak, windswept prairie, the flat horizons broken only by the odd windmill or grazing cow. The contrast with the Navajo heartland of gaping canyons and heroic spires could not be more dramatic.

A small New Mexico State Monument commemorates the site's history. The monument's manager, Gregory Scott Smith, shows up on his day off to give me a tour. He seems delighted that someone has more than casual interest. On display are a few dozen reproductions of photos of the Navajo prisoners and the fort. There's a pedestrian path astride the Pecos and a concrete block "ruin" to show where the old cavalry quarters were. A new museum building, designed by Navajo architect David Sloan, is about to be started.

"We want to include much more of the Navajo point of view," Smith tells me. "We want a balanced story."

The Army stationed a mirror signaler here on Fluted Rock, south of Canyon de Chelly, to relay messages.

THE TEARS OF BOSQUE REDONDO

Teddy Draper begins balancing the story at Navajo Fortress, *Tséláa*
in Navajo. Two geological forces, Canyon del Muerto and Black
Rock Canyon, intersect here, as do the stories, those of the white
man and of the Navajo.

"The mountains and the land between them," wrote Navajo poet George Blueeyes, "are the
only things that keep us strong."

It is the winter of 1863–64, and there is word that the soldiers will come. For months the Diné have prepared, stashing dried food atop the "fortress." Its walls are seven hundred feet of vertical slab. But there are handholds, probably left over from Anasazi times.

The soldiers camp at the base of the rock. The Navajos watch silently from above. The Diné, Teddy tells me, "make a plan—where the moon would be in a few days. They would use that [moonlight] to come down to get water."

The soldiers know Navajos are above and assume they are starving. They fry bacon to waft the aroma skyward. In Draper's story the Diné are short of water but not food. So on a night when the full moon arcs to the south, they form a human chain down the north wall of Tsélaa on yucca ropes. As the soldiers sleep, the Navajos scoop water from the creek and pass it up in a bucket brigade. "Two or three weeks later, the soldiers starve themselves," Draper says. "They got no food. So they pack up and move out."

It was a small and indecisive victory for the Navajos in a long and bitter war, but it became important in tribal lore. "We call it 'Mother Rock' in Navajo," Draper says. "This was the rebirth of Navajo, right here."

Ruth Roessel, Monty's mother, collected Draper's ancestral story and many others for a 1973 book titled *Navajo Stories of the Long Walk Period.* One story, related by tribal elder Howard W. Gorman, draws me back again and again, its heartbreak undiminished by the distance of years:

> [My] ancestors were on the long walk with their daughter, who was pregnant and about to give birth. Somewhere beyond Butterfly Mountain on this side of Belen, as it is called, south of Albuquerque, the daughter got tired and weak and couldn't keep up with the others or go any farther because of her condition… The soldiers told the parents that they had to leave their daughter behind. "Your daughter is not going to survive, anyway; sooner or later she is going to die," they said in their own language.
>
> "Go ahead," the daughter said to her parents, "things might come out all right with me." But the poor thing was mistaken… Not long after they had moved on, they heard a gunshot from where they had been a short time ago.

Carleton may have been a "dynamo of energy," but his plan for relocating an entire tribe was half-baked, absurdly naïve, and grossly

Alpine forests crown the Chuska Mountains, which provide spring
runoff for the farmers of Canyon de Chelly.

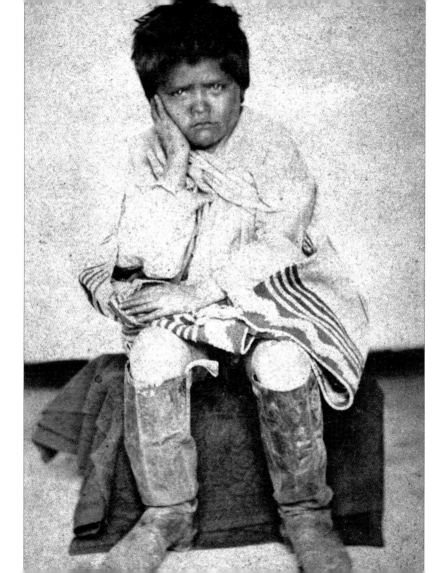

underfunded. In fairness, it wasn't entirely his fault. In 1864 the Union was still engaged in a rather larger struggle, and the Navajo problem was a flyspeck on Washington's well-heaped plate of difficulties.

Soldiers doled out food rations to the Navajos in the form of bacon or beef and flour. The meat rations were minimal and the prisoners had never seen flour before; they ate it raw or stirred it into water to form a kind of gruel. The majority of deaths likely were due to starvation, dysentery and dehydration, and exposure. From the family story of rancher Mose Denejolie, as told to Ruth Roessel:

> The U.S. Army fed corn to its horses. Then, when the horses discharged undigested corn in their manure, the Diné would dig and poke in the manure to pick out the corn that had come back out. They could be seen poking around in every corral. They made the undigested corn into meal. Plenty of hot water was used with a very small amount of corn; and it was said that hot water was the strongest of all foods.

"The Navajos were greatly delighted and expressed great satisfaction with what they saw," Captain Francis McCabe reported when the ragged convoys arrived at Fort Sumner. This seems unlikely. Food rations remained meager. No shelters had been prepared; the prisoners

A young captive, photographed at Bosque Redondo.

would have to build their own. Before the reservation land could be plowed and planted it had to be cleared of mesquite, whose roots are notoriously tangled and tenacious—a Navajo would sometimes work all day with hands and sticks to remove a single tree. Carleton's instructions to Fort Sumner's commanding officer hardly sound as if they would lead to the Navajos' "great satisfaction":

> It will require the greatest effort and most careful husbandry to keep the Indians alive until the new crop matures. Every Indian—man, woman, or child—able to dig up the ground for planting, should be kept at work every moment of the day preparing a patch, however small... Indians must live on the smallest possible quantity of food.

The Navajos worked relentlessly, both from their natural industry and from fear of starvation. That first summer three thousand acres of corn, beans, wheat, melons, and pumpkins seemed to be maturing nicely when nature unleashed an army of cutworms that devastated the corn crop, then followed with a series of October storms that destroyed half the wheat. Carleton's housing plan also collapsed through his ignorance of Navajo culture. He had envisioned a very large, "very handsome and strong" adobe town built

Navajo pot left behind at Bosque Redondo.

Navajos gathered at Bosque Redondo.

around a tree-shaded plaza, an idealized takeoff on the traditional architecture of New Mexico's Pueblo people. The Navajos, with their rural culture, had no desire to experiment with urban living. When Carleton agreed to a compromise of ten small villages, he discovered another cultural roadblock: whenever a person died inside a dwelling, no other Navajo would ever enter again.

Finally the Navajos were allowed to build their traditional hogans with whatever mesquite and cottonwood logs they could harvest from the site. After a year or two, however, they began to dismantle their own dwellings for firewood, which was becoming so scarce that finding it was a daily Long Walk in itself—as much as twelve miles. Eventually the standard Bosque Redondo architecture was a pithouse with a heap of sticks and scrap canvas forming a lop-sided and fragile roof.

In November of 1864 the Navajo population of Bosque Redondo peaked at 8,570. Navajo headman Herrero, later testifying before Congress, described conditions in the camp—with curious but typical contradictions.

Some of the soldiers do not treat us well. When at work, if we stop a little they kick us or do something else, but generally

The shade house (a temporary structure) for a modern Enemy Way ceremony, which cleanses a person after contact with an enemy. According to tribal tradition, after the Navajos returned from Bosque Redondo their corn grew poorly, but an Enemy Way ceremony helped restore the yield.

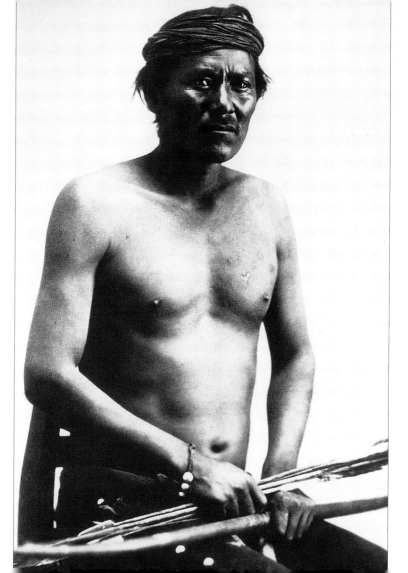

they treat us well. We do not mind if an officer punishes us, but do not like to be treated badly by the soldiers. Our women sometimes come to the tents outside the fort and make contracts with the soldiers to stay with them for a night, and give them five dollars or something else. But in the morning they take away what they gave them and kick them off. This happens most every day…the women are not forced, but consent willingly.

Prisoners would continue to dribble in for two more years as Carleton doggedly ordered more roundups, but larger numbers began to escape and tried to find their way back to northeastern Arizona. The Army had far too few soldiers to police the perimeter of a forty-square-mile camp. Carleton warned that "I will cause to be killed, every Indian I find off the reservation without a passport," but the threat failed to plug the leak.

A trek home from Bosque Redondo would take either extraordinary personal courage or supernatural intervention. Family histories brim with both. Standing on the south rim of Canyon de Chelly, Ruth Roessel and her husband, Robert, tell me how Ruth's great-grandmother, then about age fifteen, came home from Bosque Redondo:

Navajo chief Manuelito (Pistol Bullet), circa 1865–1870, Bosque Redondo.

On the night of her escape, she spoke to the Army guard dogs using their sacred names so they wouldn't bark and betray her. She walked alone and only at night for fear of being caught. The first night an owl came to her, and she followed the hooting through the night. Another night she met a bear, who guided her through the forest, her hand on its rump. Then she was threatened by a pack of hungry wolves. She spoke to them in their own language, like she had talked to the dogs. "Look at me," she cried. "I am nothing but bones. Go find a fat deer, I just want to go home."

Escapes weren't Carleton's largest problem. The Civil War ended in the spring of 1865, and Congress began to respond to a growing unease in the nation over the treatment of Indians. A Joint Special Committee began investigating (among other issues) the morass at Bosque Redondo. Crops failed again in 1865 and 1866—supernatural benevolence clearly did not extend to the Navajos' unnatural presence on the plains—and Navajos continued to die from disease and malnutrition.

Neither Navajo nor Anglo American history offers a reliable total for the number of Indians who died at or en route to Bosque

Ruins of stone corrals still stand at Bosque Redondo.

Swaddled in a chief-pattern blanket, a Navajo girl looks out over Mummy Cave in Canyon del Muerto.

Redondo. However, at the Fort Sumner monument, Gregory Scott Smith has pondered the records and extrapolated an estimate of one thousand Navajo deaths at the Bosque. In 1864, Captain McCabe filed a detailed report on the contingent he escorted from Fort Canby to Fort Sumner. He departed March 20 with 800 Navajos and collected 146 more en route. On May 11 he arrived at Fort Sumner with 788. McCabe reported that 110 had died, 25 had escaped, and "the remainder I think returned to Canby or Fort Wingate on account of inclement weather." If McCabe's contingent was typical, about 12 percent of the 11,500 Navajos who departed for Bosque Redondo died en route. That would bring the total of casualties associated with the Long Walk to 2,380—about 15 percent of the entire tribal population at the time.

In white men's history, the end of the dismal experiment at Bosque Redondo arrived in 1868. The Army and the U.S. Office of Indian Affairs had grown weary of Fort Sumner's endless requests for subsidies; clearly the reservation was never going to succeed.

On May 28, General William T. Sherman, today more famous for his Civil War march through Georgia, and Colonel Samuel F. Tappan arrived at Fort Sumner as peace commissioners to negotiate the fate of the Diné. Sherman was appalled at what he saw. "I found the bosque a mere spot of green grass in the midst of a wild desert," he wrote later, "and that the Navajos had sunk into a condition of absolute poverty and despair." Sherman and Tappan convened a meeting with seven Navajo headmen and two interpreters. Sherman first offered to send the entire tribe to Indian Territory—i.e., Oklahoma—and give them a reservation, cattle, corn, and even schools for their children. The headman Barboncito answered simply: "I hope to God you will not ask me to go to any other country except my own. It might turn out another Bosque Redondo. They told us this was a good place when we came but it is not."

Sherman was authorized to settle the issue without consulting Washington, and he wanted to cause the Navajos no more misery and his own government no more unworkable entanglements. Within two days he had drawn up a treaty with a hundred-square-mile reservation that included at least part of the Navajo homeland, in particular Canyon de Chelly and Canyon del Muerto. Barboncito greeted it with undisguised joy. "We are very well pleased with what you have said and well satisfied with that reservation. It is the very heart of our country and is more than we ever expected to get."

Navajo leader Barboncito.

At dawn on June 18, 1868, another Long Walk commenced at Fort Sumner. Fifty wagons, four Army cavalry companies, and a column of Navajos ten miles long departed, the rising sun at their backs.

THE LESSON OF BOSQUE REDONDO

Ruth Roessel drives me to the most dramatic overlook into Canyon de Chelly, where Spider Rock, a split sandstone spire, rockets eight hundred feet straight up from the canyon floor. The spire figures prominently in legend as the home of Spider Woman, who taught the Diné how to weave. Roessel brings Navajo children here to instruct them about the Long Walk. She seats them on a log, tells the stories, and lectures, "You've got to mind—because you don't want to make another mistake like a long time ago."

Mistake? My interpretation is the obvious: *The Diné shouldn't have surrendered.* But Navajo stories operate on levels that outsiders easily miss. When I read the Long Walk stories Roessel collected, I discover a strange and discomforting thread of fatalism coursing through a surprising number of them.

"The Long Walk to Fort Sumner—what was the cause of it? It began because of the behavior of a few Diné," said Howard Gorman.

Spider Rock.

He cites a Navajo named Double Face, who raided the camps of white people who were traveling west seeking gold. Double Face and others like him stole horses and killed the travelers, then feigned innocence. Henry Zah, another tribal councilman, said that the Diné back then didn't have strong leaders, so they were constantly fighting with neighboring tribes. Zah concluded that the Long Walk "was because of our own angriness."

I pay a visit to Harry Walters, a Navajo anthropologist who directs the Hatathli Museum at Diné College. He is a handsome, distinguished-looking man in his late fifties. His office décor announces that he has a foot planted in each of two worlds: a Navajo sand painting on the wall behind him, an Elvis calendar on the door.

"When my mother used to tell us the stories in the fifties, I would ask her why the Army did that to us," he tells me. "She would say, 'I guess it was up to the Diné—they were going over to the white people's settlements and raiding.' But now more and more Navajos are familiar with the true stories. If you take into consideration international laws, human rights—there was a great wrong done to us. You read today about ethnic cleansing—that's what was done to us. It was because of the white man's greed and Manifest Destiny."

Cooking breakfast for participants in an Enemy Way ceremony.

Approaching the shade house during the Enemy Way ceremony.

He speaks to me, a white man, without any apparent trace of hostility.

Later the same day I meet Johnson Dennison, a medicine man. Like Walters, Dennison's work straddles two cultures: he performs traditional healing ceremonies for patients at the Chinle hospital after the modern doctors have given their best efforts. He also has a degree in educational administration from the University of New Mexico. I

Later, participants in the ceremony will eat this mutton.

sense a vivid intelligence behind eyes that seem constantly to be prob-
ing, testing me. But he is friendly and patient with his explanations.

He starts at the beginning, literally:

The Navajo people have a story: There were First Man and
First Woman, and they migrated from the first to the second
world, and then the third and fourth world. Everywhere
there was disharmony. And people were just moving away
from their problems.

Then they found out that relationships were the key to living in harmony: relationship with self, relationship with the
earth, relationships with neighbors. First Woman instructed
them to live in good relationships always. They began living
in harmony, and that's how the Navajo people came about.

I ask how the Navajo creation story relates to the Long Walk.
Dennison nearly echoes Howard Gorman's words: *It began because of
the behavior of a few Diné.* "At the time of the Long Walk, people were
doing whatever they wanted. There was no order. People were doing
all kinds of things: raiding, making war, killing each other. They were
out of harmony. The Long Walk brought us back together."

Late Classic Navajo serape, circa 1865–1872, likely made for sale to soldiers at Bosque Redondo. Such beautiful work, done under such harsh conditions, demonstrates a power of the human spirit much beyond mere survival.

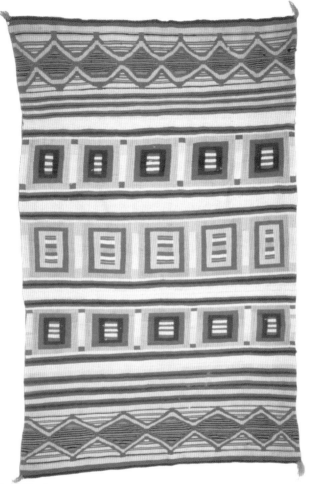

Late Classic Navajo serape, circa 1860–1865, woven of raveled and commercial 3-ply yarns (pinks and reds all dyed with cochineal) that were probably obtained through government annuities provided to the weaver at Bosque Redondo.

There is no longer a monolithic Navajo view of the Long Walk—the Diné today get their information from universities, libraries, the Internet, and their grandmothers. Small wonder the stories seem laced with contradictions. (And almost predictably, before we finish, Dennison tells me: "It was not the Navajos who started it. The Europeans were the ones who took our people as slaves.") It can be frustrating for an outsider trying to discover the underlying truth—but then I remind myself that we white people have always looked at Indian cultures wanting, and expecting, simple answers. James Carleton was not the first to make this mistake, and certainly not the last.

White America's attitude toward the earlier inhabitants of our shared continent has whipsawed through several course corrections, each of them extreme. First was contempt for the

A 1910 portrait of Hastiin-Nez, who as a boy carried his two-year-old brother on the Long Walk. When E. A. Burbank painted his portrait, Hastiin-Nez was the chief cook at the Hubbell Trading Post at Ganado.

Indians as an "inferior race," which formed the moral justification for their removal or extermination. In the late nineteenth century came patronizing benevolence, a widely shared belief that Indian cultures could achieve great things when "helped" to learn white ways and adopt white religion. The Reverend Jedediah Morse set the tone in a report on U.S. Indian policy. Indians, Morse wrote,

Rock art in Canyon de Chelly stretches from early Basketmaker times, possibly 2,000 years ago, to modern Navajo. This Navajo pictograph panel above Standing Cow Ruin depicts a Spanish cavalcade circa 1805.

This turquoise bracelet was made in a style of silverwork that dates from the Long Walk era.

were "an intelligent and noble part of our race, and capable of high moral and intellectual improvement." In the twentieth century came racism and, most recently, obsequious political correctness.

Some Navajos believe this rockfall at Black Mesa predicted the Long Walk, but it was recognized as an omen only after the Navajos returned.

I am happy to have spent enough time among the Navajos to understand that none of these views is accurate or realistic. Navajo culture is neither inferior nor superior to white America's; it is merely different. Both cultures are capable of incredible foolishness and cruelty; both of astounding insights and achievements.

The irony—no, the lesson—of the Long Walk is that it preserved Navajo identity instead of destroying it. The Navajos returned to their land with a new and deeper bond to it, and the stories tightened the fiber that held the culture together. The tribe today numbers more than 200,000 members, and the Navajo Nation is the largest reservation in the United States.

"The appreciation of the land, the language, the culture, the ceremonies—we almost lost this," says Harry Walters. "I don't want to say it was good that the Long Walk happened. It's like hitting yourself over the head with a hammer: it feels so good when you stop. But it's what made us strong."

Juanita, wife of Navajo chief Manuelito, photographed in 1874.

Dawn, contemporary Enemy Way ceremony.

Johnson Dennison wonders. The medicine man surveys the modern troubles of the Diné and sees disharmony—things falling apart, the center failing to hold. "It's been more than 130 years, and people are acting like they didn't learn anything. Every day someone dies because of alcohol. There are all kinds of social problems. We are not teaching the old ways. We are not practicing the right way of living.

"But the weapon we need to overcome all these problems, we already have it. All we need is to rediscover who we are."

This rock mound honors the sacrifice made by Navajos who took part in the Long Walk, and it continues to grow. A Navajo family explained its significance to the author and invited him to place a rock on it, too.

PLACES TO VISIT
IN AND AROUND NAVAJO COUNTRY

CANYON DE CHELLY NATIONAL MONUMENT, Chinle, Arizona, 928-674-5500. Visitors may hike unescorted into the canyon on only one trail, the White House Ruin. For a better tour of the Canyon, sign up with a Navajo guide at the Monument Visitors Center or Thunderbird Lodge, 800-679-2473.

CANYONLANDS NATIONAL PARK, southeastern Utah, 435-719-2313. Protects one of the last relatively undisturbed areas of the Colorado Plateau—a landscape of canyons, mesas, and deep river gorges.

CHACO CULTURE NATIONAL HISTORICAL PARK, northwestern New Mexico, 505-786-7014. Preserves archaeological sites in the sacred homeland of Pueblo, Hopi, and Navajo people.

FORT SUMNER STATE MONUMENT, Fort Sumner, New Mexico, 505-355-2573. Includes a museum and interpretive trail.

FOUR CORNERS NATIONAL MONUMENT, where you can stand in Colorado, Utah, Arizona, and New Mexico at the same time.

GOULDING'S LODGE, southeastern Utah, 435-727-3231, also includes Goulding's Museum and Trading Post (housed in the original 1920s building), a campground, and tours of the area given by Navajo guides.

GRAND STAIRCASE-ESCALANTE NATIONAL MONUMENT, southern Utah, 435-644-4300, features 1.9 million acres of rugged, multi-hued geological formations.

HUBBELL TRADING POST NATIONAL HISTORIC SITE, Ganado, Arizona, 928-755-3475. Established in 1878, this federal site also has a working general store, with a stunning collection of Navajo rugs, jewelry, and other crafts for sale.

MONUMENT VALLEY TRIBAL PARK, southeastern Utah, 435-727-5874. Guided and self-guided tours of one of the most photographed places on earth; visitor center with gift shop.

MUSEUM OF NORTHERN ARIZONA, Flagstaff, Arizona, 928-779-1527. An excellent museum dedicated to the natural history and human cultures of the Colorado Plateau.

NAVAJO NATIONAL MONUMENT, near Kayenta, Arizona, 928-672-2700. Anasazi ruins; advance plans essential to visit. Tours to ruins in summer only.

NAVAJO TRIBAL MUSEUM, Window Rock, Arizona, 928-871-7941. Permanent collection includes a comprehensive photographic display on the Long Walk.

NAVAJO VETERANS MEMORIAL PARK, Window Rock, Arizona. Symbolic structures honoring Navajos who served in the U.S. military, at the base of Window Rock geological formation.

PETRIFIED FOREST NATIONAL PARK, east-central Arizona, 928-524-6228. Colorful petrified wood and the multi-hued badlands of the Painted Desert.

RECOMMENDED READING

Heisey, Adriel, and Kenji Kawano. *In the Fifth World: Portrait of the Navajo Nation.* Tucson, Arizona: Rio Nuevo Publishers, 2001.

Iverson, Peter, and Monty Roessel (photographer). *Diné: A History of the Navajos.* Albuquerque, New Mexico: University of New Mexico Press, 2002.

Kosik, Fran. *Native Roads: Motoring Guide to the Navajo and Hopi Nations.* Tucson, Arizona: Rio Nuevo Publishers, 2000.

Locke, Raymond Friday. *The Book of the Navajo.* Los Angeles, California: Holloway House Publishing Co., 1976.

McClain, Sally. *Navajo Weapon: The Navajo Code Talkers.* Tucson, Arizona: Rio Nuevo Publishers, 2001.

Roessel, Robert A. Jr. *Pictorial History of the Navajo from 1860 to 1910.* Rough Rock, Arizona: Navajo Curriculum Center Press, 1988.

Roessel, Ruth. *Navajo Stories of the Long Walk Period.* Tsaile, Arizona: Diné College Press, 1999.

Trimble, Stephen. *The People: Indians of the American Southwest.* Santa Fe, New Mexico: School of American Research Press, 1993.

White, Richard. *It's Your Misfortune and None of My Own: A New History of the American West.* Norman, Oklahoma: University of Oklahoma Press, 1991.

PHOTOGRAPHY © AS FOLLOWS: